COUNT THE DIGGERS, DUMPER TRUCKS & TRACTORS!

Volume 1

Warning: Fun ahead!

Welcome to Vol. 1!

COUNT, OBSERVE AND HAVE FUN
LEARNING ALL ABOUT THESE
AMAZING CONSTRUCTION
VEHICLES AND OBJECTS!

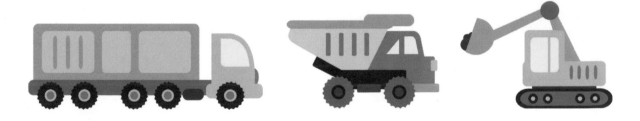

Best of luck!

© NCBUSA
PUBLICATIONS

Count the dumper trucks!

There are three dumper trucks!

3

How many bulldozers can you see here?

There is only

bulldozer!

Can you see
more traffic cones or
more roadblocks?

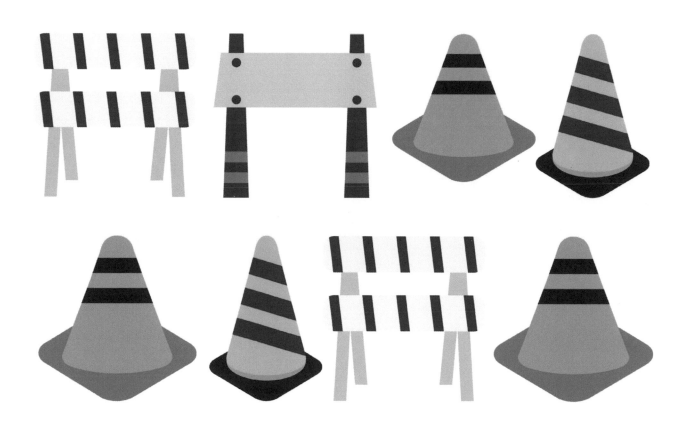

There are

5 and 3

traffic cones   roadblocks

So there are more traffic cones than roadblocks!

How many forklifts can you find?

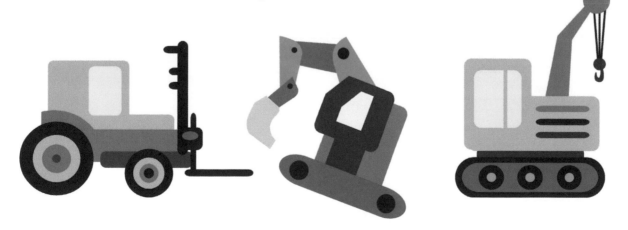

There are two forklifts!

Forklifts are used to carry heavy materials!

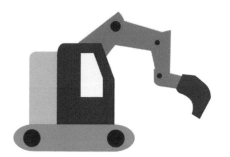

How many
diggers
are here?

There are

diggers!

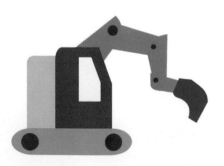 

How many cranes are there here?

There is only one crane!

Cranes are named after birds!

How many tractors can you count?

There are

2

tractors!

Tractors are most often
used on farms!

How many tankers can you count?

There are

5 tankers!

Tankers carry petrol, oil, chemicals and other liquids!

Can you count more excavators or more concrete mixers here?

There are

4

4

So there are the same
number of both vehicles!

Count the traffic cones!

How many
pickup trucks
can you find?

There are four pickup trucks.

Did you count correctly?

How many construction signs can you see here?

There are

8

construction signs!

Are there more tractors or more roadblocks below?

There are

4 and **2**

tractors   roadblocks

So there are more
tractors than roadblocks!

How did you do?

How many grey trucks are there?

There are

2

grey trucks!

We hope that you and your child/children have enjoyed learning to count with this book!

IF YOU HAVE - A GLOWING REVIEW ON AMAZON WOULD BE MUCH APPRECIATED.

What's next?

Get our full series of counting (and coloring) books!

To purchase - just search 'NCBUSA Publications'

We are also extremely excited to be publishing our first **digger story book**, releasing in April 2021. You can get your copy for FREE by going to _ncbusa-publications.com_ & joining our email list, where we'll let you know about new construction books we publish!

Printed in Great Britain
by Amazon